JAPANESE MYTHOLOGY

Tsukuyomi

BY EMMA KAISER

CONTENT CONSULTANT
LAURA NÜFFER, PhD
ASSISTANT PROFESSOR OF EAST ASIAN STUDIES
COLBY COLLEGE

Kids Core
An Imprint of Abdo Publishing
abdobooks.com

abdobooks.com

Printed in the United States of America, North Mankato, Minnesota.
102024
012025

THIS BOOK CONTAINS RECYCLED MATERIALS

Cover Photo: Shutterstock Images
Interior Photos: Shutterstock Images, 4–5, 7, 12–13, 18, 20–21, 22, 28 (bottom), 29 (top), 29 (bottom); Hiko Photography/Shutterstock Images, 9, 28 (top); John W. Banagan/Stone/Getty Images, 10; Nelson Mendoza/Alamy, 14; Red Line Editorial, 16; Susumu Yoshioka/DigitalVision/Getty Images, 17; Jim Kruger/E+/Getty Images, 24; Science History Images/Alamy, 25; imagenavi/Getty Images, 26

Editor: Christa Kelly
Series Designer: Ryan Gale

Library of Congress Control Number: 2024938335

Publisher's Cataloging-in-Publication Data

Names: Kaiser, Emma, author.
Title: Tsukuyomi / by Emma Kaiser
Description: Minneapolis, Minnesota: ABDO Publishing, 2025 | Series: Japanese mythology | Includes online resources and index.
Identifiers: ISBN 9781098296001 (lib. bdg.) | ISBN 9798384917007 (ebook)
Subjects: LCSH: Mythology, Japanese--Juvenile literature. | Deities--Juvenile literature. | Gods, Japanese--Juvenile literature. | Moon (in religion, folk-lore, etc.)--Juvenile literature. | Moon--Folklore--Juvenile literature. | Mythology, Asian--Juvenile literature.
Classification: DDC 398.21--dc23

CONTENTS

Although Tsukuyomi, *pictured*, and Amaterasu were very different, they still loved each other.

CHAPTER 1

The Legend of the Sun and the Moon

The Japanese goddess of the sun and the god of the moon once ruled the heavens together. The sun goddess was named Amaterasu (pronounced ah-mah-teh-rah-soo). Her name means "Great Goddess Lighting Up Heaven."

Amaterasu's brother was the moon god Tsukuyomi (soo-koo-yo-mee). Tsukuyomi was also bright and shining. But he did not shine as brightly as his sister.

Amaterasu and Tsukuyomi lived in the heavens. Other gods lived on Earth. One day, Amaterasu heard about a goddess on Earth named Ukemochi (oo-kay-moh-chee). Ukemochi was the goddess of food. Amaterasu told her brother to visit the goddess.

When Tsukuyomi arrived on Earth, Ukemochi prepared a feast for him. But she prepared the feast in a strange way. First, she faced the fields and spit rice out of her mouth. Then she faced the sea and spit out fish. Then she faced the mountains and spit out meat.

Amaterasu is often considered Japan's most important god.

Tsukuyomi was disgusted. He thought that Ukemochi was insulting him. Tsukuyomi was so angry that he killed Ukemochi. As Ukemochi lay dead, new plants and animals sprang from her body. Beans and wheat appeared. Horses and cows appeared too.

Amaterasu was furious when she heard that Tsukuyomi had murdered Ukemochi. She called Tsukuyomi evil and wicked. She swore

Kojiki

Kojiki is the oldest known book from Japan. It was written in 712 CE. Its name means "Record of Ancient Matters." The earliest story about Tsukuyomi comes from *Kojiki*. More stories about Tsukuyomi come from another old book called *Nihon Shoki*.

Japan is one of many countries that has stories explaining why day and night are separate.

she would never see him again. From that day forward, Amaterasu refused to share the sky with Tsukuyomi. This is why the sun only shines during the day and the moon only shines at night.

People in Japan have been practicing Shinto for more than 1,000 years.

Japanese Mythology

Japan is a country in eastern Asia. Many people in Japan practice a religion called Shinto. The word *Shinto* means "way of the gods." Shinto centers around *kami*, or "spirits." Gods are kami. So are some other supernatural creatures. Mountains, trees, and rocks can be kami too.

Stories are important in Shinto. Some Shinto stories explain how the world was created. Others talk about gods and heroes. Still others explain natural events, such as why day and night exist.

There are very few myths about Tsukuyomi. He is mysterious. Many people in Japan consider him a minor god. But the moon god still fascinates people around the world.

Further Evidence

Look at the website below. Does it give any new evidence to support Chapter One?

Japan

abdocorelibrary.com/tsukuyomi

Izanagi, *left*, traveled to Yomi to find his dead wife, Izanami, *right*.

CHAPTER 2

The Birth of the Moon God

Once there was a god named Izanagi. One day, Izanagi journeyed to Yomi, the land of the dead. When Izanagi returned from the land of the dead, he was unclean. He dove into a river to bathe.

People have different ideas about what Tsukuyomi looks like.

As Izanagi washed himself, the sun goddess Amaterasu was born from his left eye. Izanagi continued washing, and Tsukuyomi was born from his right eye. After that, a third god was born from Izanagi's nose. This god was named Susanoo (soo-sah-no-oh).

Izanagi was proud of the children he had created. He gave them different **realms** to rule. He told Amaterasu to rule the heavens. He told Tsukuyomi to rule the night. Finally, he told Susanoo to rule the sea and storms.

Moon Reading

The name *Tsukuyomi* translates to "moon reading." In ancient times, people used the moon's phases to keep track of the months. This was sometimes called moon reading.

Writing *Tsukuyomi*

月読

月 = Moon

読 = Read

The Japanese language uses different letters than English. Each letter represents a sound. Japanese also uses symbols called *kanji*. Two kanji make up the name Tsukuyomi.

Ruler of the Night

As the moon god, Tsukuyomi ruled the night. He also ruled the ocean tides. This is because the moon controls the tides.

Rice is the most commonly grown crop in Japan.

Tsukuyomi is also linked to farming. This is because the moon shows the passing months. This helps farmers know when to plant crops.

People in Japan still worship Ukemochi today.

The moon god could be violent. He killed Ukemochi. But he also helped people. After he killed the goddess of food, plants and animals sprouted from her body. Thanks to Tsukuyomi, humans could grow crops.

Primary Source

An ancient Japanese book called *Nihon Shoki* describes what Amaterasu said after Tsukuyomi killed Ukemochi:

> Amaterasu . . . said "[You are] a wicked **deity**. I must not see [you] face to face." So they were separated by one day and one night and **dwelt** apart.

Source: W.G. Aston, translator. *Nihongi: Chronicles of Japan from the Earliest Times to A.D.* Kegan Paul, Trench, Trübner & Co., Limited, 1896, p. 32. Internet Archive, archive.org.

Comparing Texts

Does this quote support the information in this chapter? Or does it give a different perspective? Explain how in a few sentences.

When people visit shrines dedicated to Tsukuyomi, they are visiting the god himself.

CHAPTER 3

Honoring the Moon God

Across Japan, there are thousands of **shrines**. These shrines are dedicated to different Shinto gods. There are more than 80 shrines to Tsukuyomi.

The most important shrine to Tsukuyomi is the Matsunoo Taisha shrine. This shrine is in Kyoto.

The gates in front of Shinto shrines are called *torii.*

It was built in 701 CE. This makes it one of the oldest shrines in the city. The Matsunoo Taisha shrine is known for the giant red gate at its entrance.

Tsukimi

Tsukuyomi is not as celebrated as his siblings. He is rarely honored in art or theater. However, Japanese people perform many traditions to honor the moon itself. *Tsukimi* is one of these traditions. The word *tsukimi* means "moon viewing." The full moon in autumn is very bright and beautiful. Every year, Japanese people celebrate this beautiful moon. This tradition has been practiced for more than 1,000 years.

The Rabbit in the Moon

Not all Japanese myths about the moon center on Tsukuyomi. One myth describes a nice rabbit who was brought to the moon. It lives high above the Earth and spends its time making rice cakes called *mochi*. People in Japan say the dark spots of the moon resemble this rabbit.

Many people call the bright autumn moon the harvest moon.

Some Japanese people put out special decorations for tsukimi. Susuki grass is a **traditional** decoration. It is a tall grass with

In the 700s, tsukimi was celebrated among wealthy people. By the 1600s, tsukimi was popular among commoners too.

feathery plumes. Foods **harvested** in autumn such as chestnuts and sweet potatoes are also used as decorations.

Poetry used to be a popular part of tsukimi. Japanese people would hold tsukimi parties. At these parties, they wrote poems about the moon. Some Japanese people still do this. Other people just enjoy the moon with their friends.

According to tradition, eating *tsukimi dango* brings health and happiness.

During tsukimi, some people enjoy rice dumplings called *tsukimi dango*. These dumplings are round and white. They look like little moons.

Though Tsukuyomi is not as celebrated as his siblings, he is still known as a powerful kami. His story has been told for more than a thousand years. Today, he remains a fascinating character in Shinto mythology.

Explore Online

Visit the website below. Does it give any new information about tsukimi that wasn't in Chapter Three?

Tsukimi

abdocorelibrary.com/tsukuyomi

Legendary Facts

Tsukuyomi is the Shinto god of the moon.

Tsukuyomi was born from the right eye of the god Izanagi.

The sun goddess Amaterasu and the storm god Susanoo are Tsukuyomi's siblings.

Tsukuyomi is honored at shrines across Japan.

Glossary

deity
a god or goddess

dwelt
lived

harvested
picked or gathered, especially relating to crops

realms
places that a person controls, such as kingdoms or empires

shrine
a place where gods and other religious figures are honored and worshiped

traditional
relating to practices from the past

Online Resources

To learn more about Tsukuyomi and Japanese mythology, visit our free resource websites below.

Core Library
CONNECTION
FREE! COMMON CORE MULTIMEDIA RESOURCES

Visit **abdocorelibrary.com** or scan this QR code for free Common Core resources for teachers and students, including vetted activities, multimedia, and booklinks, for deeper subject comprehension.

Booklinks
NONFICTION NETWORK
FREE! ONLINE NONFICTION RESOURCES

Visit **abdobooklinks.com** or scan this QR code for free additional online weblinks for further learning. These links are routinely monitored and updated to provide the most current information available.

Learn More

Fox, Jay. *My First Book of Japanese*. Bushel & Peck, 2022.

Golkar, Golriz. *Amaterasu*. Abdo, 2025.

Van, R. L. *Japan*. Abdo, 2023.

Index

About the Author

Emma Kaiser is a writer and educator based in western Minnesota. She has a master of fine arts in creative writing from the University of Minnesota, and her writing has appeared in several magazines and publications. She is also the author of a number of nonfiction books for students.